The Great Global Anthology Vol-1

Pentupthoughts

About Book

Pentupthoughts presents its second anthology "The Great Global Anthology". This is a combined effort of writers across the globe. The theme was kept open and we received several poems. The Anthology has diverse poems and that's what we at PENT-UP THOUGHTS strive for. We welcome all kinds of works going beyond personal lyric to touching contemporary issues.

I can understand that there has been a great delay in publishing this anthology. I sincerely apologize for this delay.

We would like to thank all the participants who have been included in this anthology.

- Zai (Founder) Pentupthoughts

Designed and edited by Zai-ul-haq (pentupthoughts)

Printed by Notionpress

If you want to edit, design or publish your own book email us
pentupthoughts4@gmail.com

Our publishing package starts from Rs. 499 Kindle Ebook

Rs. 1499(without book cover) and Rs.1999(with book cover) Paperback only

Rs.2999 paperback with book cover+ Ebook(promotion on pentupthoghts)

Contributors

Deeksha Raina

Devguni

Sheikh Fajar

Dr Sadiya Sultana

Aarzoo Agarwal

Siddhi

Sthuti

Ishita chatterjee

Mz

Aheli Bhattacherjee

Sristi Anupam

Anu Fildha

Swastika Mukherjee

Amian Bent

Sampreeti Kale

Mohua Chakraborty

Zaara Ali

Srishti

Roopal Aroora

Dina Mohammed

Sue seth

Tanya Verma

Nikitha senny

Khatija Khan

Hridya shrama

Sani zehra

PR Augustina Mahanta

Sarab Bawa

Sharli

Kajal

<u>Muted.</u>

It is odd

for I haven't really been;

for a long time now.

Yet here I am, baring my soul,

an audience of spectacled strangers

under the moonlit night

in front of open mics.

Is it odd,

how easily you praise the words

yet here I am, still,

unable to fathom the depth of it all.

I wonder if now,

It's just melancholy

for I don't hope no more,

all I hear in your thundering encore

is my aloofness reverberating through?

-Deeksha Raina

About Poet/writer

A software engineer and a passionate writer, Deeksha began writing at the age of 15 and since then has published a novel titled 'It was Love' and numerous poems/short stories as part of anthologies of diverse genres. She has been in on various open mics, national level poetry competitions and has been invited for book reading events. Recently, she compiled an anthology titled Chasing Hope! under Rosewood Publication. it's available on Amazon and Flipkart.

Monday mournful mornings you mock my dodgy self as

it fails to cast a spell on your hungry self.

Guess my butterfingers and your equilibrium breaks the delicate glass of love.

Tuesday tattered times you spit toxic loud angsty

syllables as it fails to reach the expectations you have had for me now and then.

Guess my dumb brain and your prodigy brain can't find peace on intricated sites

Wednesday worn-out days of the week when you subtly compare my faults and her beauty with constant chanting to your deity how you wish me to be like her all the time.

Guess my beastly benign body and her boisterous beautiful body makes you bow in the wrong direction Thursday tainted times your effort words succumb to my melancholic screams.

In the name of relief, I pen it on torn pieces of crushed papers every night.

Friday fainted day you call me filthy names, frame my name into filthy blocks.

Your insolvency dominates the gullibility of my timid flowers with your thorny bushes.

Saturday sorrows swirl in all the corners, reminding me that I'm a liability and you're an asset as equity sits on your lap and the sheet seems to be unbalanced on the utmost vitality of the subtle life of broken hearts.

Sunday smells rotten because of the weekly treacherous but now it's also habitual.

You walk away in the blue and I'm still in the blue because you say I deserve the bad blue.

I boom in my blues for an hour or two.

You bring back your blues reminding me of the bad blues and things to come over again.

And seven adds to thirty and thirty adds to three hundred sixty five and booms blooms with each passing time.

- Devguni.

About Poet/writer

Hello, I am Devguni. I am a 23-year-old girl from the City of Temples, Jammu. I've always been enthusiastic about writing which steered my curiosity in reading. I like to make inferences about what I read and what the author wants to imply. I love to write about everything in general and lately trying my hands on every kind of writing style and I wish to explore more in the field of writing because more is always good.

" The strange bond"

When you get hardships in life,

Then my heart also aches

When you suffer in life,

Then I also feel that pain

But perhaps I don't care for you,

There's just an unusual bond between us

I'm so busy in your love that

without hearing your voice,I can't sleep

Without seeing your face,I don't get peace

Without feeling your essence,I don't get relief

But perhaps still I don't care for you,

There's just an unusual bond between us

- Sheikh Fajar

About Poet/writer

Sheikh Fajar is an eminent writer from the valley of Kashmir who pens poems about love , compassion, kindness and nature of human hearts.She has co-authored several books and is the author of the e-book"Longings of the Sacred heart".She has been selected for IBR 2022 for her writings.

Poverty yet Purity

Living in those kachha houses,

limited things their life comprises.

Being content is what they learnt

all through the past to the current.

Their houses might be small,

yet biggest are their hearts.

Whoever might be the achiever,

they celebrate happiness together.

A single family they belong to

despite living in different huts of bamboo.

They believe in caring and sharing

Purest souls they're, who can never be faking

- Dr Sadiya Sultana

About Poet/Writer

This is Dr Sadiya Sultana, a practising Indian doctor. Writing serves as a medium to express freely all that I could never dare to speak. I get to see the society from a closer perspective as a doctor, and I write focusing on the social issues that prevail among people I meet. I write aiming to spread positivity around and to heal people through palliative words.

'To Be or Not To Be', that is the question Shakespeare wrote years back,

But till today, I ask myself, To do or not to do? To Be or Not To Be?

To swim across the ocean and drench myself, to quest my thirst of knowing what lies on the other side, Or just to sit and live an unknown life.

To jump from the aeroplane and feel myself, to understand how it really feels to let it go, Or just simply hold the bucket of guilt till my hand turns yellow.

To wear my heart on the sleeve and allow it to be vulnerable, to know what love is,

Or just let it be tied with a tape and know what hate is.

To soak in all the sun and let my skin breathe, to know that distance and admiration are in no relation to each other,

Or just let my fingers to obstruct the light and wait for years to uncover.

To keep chasing the one who isn't walking steps for me, to be unconditional in every way, Or just have one more piece of my jigsaw heart.

To keep gazing the moon and its spots, to realise that it is okay to have flaws,

Or just never know that defects also deserve applause.

To keep speaking love and considering it to be not for sale,

Or just let my lips turn pale.

To be a dreamer, believer, achiever,

Or to be in the enigmatic utopia that exists in paradise.

To take a step forward and know that,

Or take a step backwards and be an escaper.

-Aarzoo Agarwal

<u>December</u>

The only month
Full of sorrow and joy,
Of hopeless nights and
brighter days,
Laughing at one moment
and other can make you cry,

The only month
When it feels like both
the beginning and the end,
The end of past pain making
us strong for future rain,
The hope of orphans and unfathered fruits,

The only month

When earth itself has frozen,

When children reside inside,

and snow! snow! everywhere outside,

the sky become hazy by the fog's layer,

Their mothers wrap them within blankets,

Enjoying their holidays wearing their favourite jackets.

What old December's bareness everywhere!

- Siddhi

About Poet/writer

Siddhi is 18 year old. An aspiring writer who loves to read. An optimistic person who believes that man is the creator of his own destiny.

I HOPE THIS POEM FINDS YOU

I hope this poem finds you
when you are trying to
mend your broken heart,
heal your gaping wound
and supress your enduring pain.
I hope this poem finds you
when you are doubting your self-worth
because of the scars someone left on you.
when the chaos and madness inside your head
doesn't seem to end.
when the restlessness building up in you
has become a valley of thoughts and emotions now.
when agony runs through your veins,
incessantly, that you can't sleep for the blink of an eye.

I hope this poem finds you
when you miss someone who you know will not come back,
but the "why" of it haunts you all night.
when your life is drowned in darkness
and you are all alone, in search of light.
when things are not going your way
and you feel like giving up.

I hope this poem finds you

to give you strength and say to you that,

"It is going to be okay.

" I hope this poem finds you

in the way you would find your happiness.

-Sthuti

<u>**IN THE POETRIES OF HEART BREAKS**</u>

When the curtains are drawn and the world falls unconscious,
your memories awaken and drive my sleep away.
My lips prompt a hundred unanswered questions
that my eyes manifest in the form of tears.
The soft touch of your hands that once fondled my longings
slipped away no sooner than the sand grains caught in hand do.

The voices in my head are tired to scream anymore.
They have now built a castle at the corner of my mind
and decided to silently reside there budging to not go
away, unlike the way you did.
Pain has wrapped itself around my skin.
Vows of infinite ties and dreams,
turned into ruins of hoax and betrayal.

I often look at the stars above and wonder
if the love that once shone in your eyes was a reflection of a true sentiment
or just a mirage of your love in my head that perhaps never existed.
While you were here, you sealed my lips with favorite colors of my heart.
And when you left, you painted the same heart with the lies of your lips.

Your love was surely fleeting,

for it took moments of a shooting star to collapse my heart

and turn it into nothing more than suffering wrapped in blood coated tissue cells.

The night ends, but the feeling doesn't.

Oh darling! How I wish you knew that I still write about

you in my writings. Earlier in the poetries of love, today in those of heart breaks.

-Sthuti

About Poet/writer

Sthuti, who is currently pursuing her B.Com, is an enthusiastic, open minded and easy going person, who takes interests in writing poetries and reading books. She is someone who is intrigued by the play of words in literature.

'Nights year old'

We're nights year old.

From running out of breath

while sharing details of our days,

in hushed low voices.

Froth moistening our microphones.

Under the shared cozy blanket with my grandma,

I lay.

With you ; on the other side of the cell-phone.

You say, "Dream with me" ;

and we depart on a midnight ride,

dreaming carelessly.

Your voice like a midnight lullaby.

You carry me to the other side,
with you.

In your serenity

it's TIMELESS.

I don't wanna breathe into life.

There's a history beyond us.

Rivers of memories to flow.

Till waking up to each - other's snores.

We've grown - up together.

Yeah! We're nights year old.

-Ishita Chatterjee

It is in this way that i love you

never in secrecy nor in pride

for i have found no other way

than to deem in my existence

throught the breath that leaves your body

only to be mine

carrying but a trace of your sweet fragrance

that wraps tightly around my beating heart

and i fall slowly on your grounds

like the heavy drops of silent rain

fragile and complete

-MZ

<u>**What is Love**</u>

Let this be my way to hue; the words that seek solace,

My tale of life; brimming in love: had hued me with its grace.

Walking past the era of tech; dealing in robo men,

Love is but in cyberspace; a game of agile brains.

Chatting o'er the virtual white, on instagram they say,

Love unfurls in codes entwined; hued in white and grey.

Facebook brings us close to hearts; I don't! But they feel,

The ones who brim in eternal faith and drench in virtual zeal.

Love for me; if at all you ask, I shall say for sure

Is not just touch but the unheard words, too sublime and too pure.

It speaks for souls; not for bods that meander o'er the crust,

Love is pristine as the air and ubiquitous as the dust.

Love hath never pulled a string betwixt the race and creed,

Love hath never proclaimed share on codes of filthy greed.

Love can sprinkle bliss and peace from the cerulean clouds,

Love can make us feel lonesome even amid the crowds.

Love is pristine as the Geeta; pure as quoran,

Love hath preached the spells of truth beneath the ablaze sun.

Love hath breathed in dawn's azaan and evenings divine nymph,

Love hath kissed the baptised souls through words from bible's crimp.

Love hath ruled through the yore and into the cosmos grids,

Love hath blossomed in petals of bliss and kissed the wounded breeds.

Love hath ne'er bruised the souk for mundane greed for wealth,

Love hath bestowed sublime elixirs to adorn with gems of health.

Let love flutter as falcon's wings to win the abysmal sky,

Let not hatred parch the wings before they learn to fly.

Love can heal the gangrenes of sin and cleanse the mortal lands,

Tis indeed the game of souls and tis always in our hands.

- Aheli Bhattacherjee

About Poet/writer

Aheli Bhattacherjee was born on 12th October 2005, in the city of mixed cultures,
Asansol. She is a sixteen year-old girl, who is a school going student reading in class 10.
She was greatly inspired by her Chemistry teacher, Ms.P.Banerjee(whom she loves just
like her mother), to be strong and to face the complexities of life with ease. Aheli took
up writing poems as a hobby when she was 11 years old. She hopes to bring about
radical change in the minds of people about their frequent and undefined emotions. She
gave writing poetry anthology a start, by penning down her feelings and experiences.

Gazing through the window of my car

Half asleep, humming the song

Suddenly

A familiar lane enraptured me.

It was the street I used to

Walk down in my teens.

The street was once reminiscent

And still powerful to

Send me into nostalgia.

It's been so long.

The familiar lane was not familiar anymore.

The road which I used to escape from the world,

Is now like a stranger to me.

The bare tree I used to

Have a long conversation with,

I can't find it anymore.

It was not the chilly winter morning,

But the overwhelming joy

Of being there once again

Left me quivering.

The street whose beauty couldn't be resisted,

even by the moon.

Is now a concrete jungle.

The silent road is now lost in cluster.

And in the crowd,

My mind was anticipating

to see the sixteen years old girl

Roaming around, talking to

Nobody but herself

Accompanied by the moon.

-Sristi Anupam

About Poet/writer

She is a scribbler who likes to transform her imagination into words. A Potterhead studying medicine in Ambala. She believes in enhancing knowledge & new experiences are always welcomed.

Louder heart beats,

Shaking hands,

Sweating forehead,

A rose in his hand.

Reciting those words

Right from his heart,

Wishing for her acceptance,

With tears in his eyes,

He says," I miss you a lot,

Are you alright?"

And he lays the black rose,

Infront of the words,

"A lovely mother,

And a dearly wife,

May you rest in peace, my life."

-Anu Fildha

<u>**The Pages Of The Book**</u>

At eight o'clock in the evening, when I was a distracted little child,

The pages of the book prevented my mind from flying wild.

On a sweet summer morning, when I wanted to just play,

The pages of the book gripped me in their engaging, learned spell.

Under the blanket in chilly winters, when I wished to sleep some more,

The pages of the book met my eyes and said, "Today's discomfort is tomorrow's high
score".....

Dark, in my room, when I cried mercilessly for my faith was sold,

The pages of the book touched my palms, preventing my heart from freezing cold.

Through freckles and knuckles every time I went through,

The pages of my books had comforted me with warmth,

Convinced me that it's better to be alone than lonely,

In their caress I discovered- few is a braver word than new.

-Swastika Mukherjee

About Poet/writer

I am Swastika Mukherjee, eighteen years old, figuring out life! This journey is blissful and blasphemous, depending upon the roads we travel through! Hold my hand along the adventures of youth and the tribulations of being yourself.... Follow me @ink_n_whispers for more soulful poetry!

A Portrait of Me

Countless vices spread upon my face
Like a portrait painted only in shades
Of dead black and mummified grey
I peel them back (with a monumental effort)
To gaze upon the skin within
But I find nothing
Nothing but a canvas of brittle bones
Sapped out of energizing life
And injected with the world's favourite drink,
A simple concoction of detachment and apathy
I put the vices back in their place
At least they give the appearance
That I feel something (even if it is baseless cruelty)

As time passes by, the vices grow thick
Layering me in a coat of bitterness
(And longing I suppressed underneath)
Until I am bloated, bulging
My body, a single stretch of bee-stung skin
Red is now all I see, red is all I feel
And it seeps in, right into the bones
Causing a blaze inside that I cannot control

So I burn in silence

Pain searing through my nerves like blood

Giving birth to the deadliest sin in my very heart

And now, my vice-ladden skin falls off

A mass of inflamed flesh and gore

Leaving my true self to be seen by the world

But I dare not look at it

For I am afraid that if I do

I will find something darker than Dorian Gray did.

-Amian Bent

About Poet/writer

A 21 year old undergrad student who loves to write as a way to express the emotions
that cannot be articulated by speaking. Lover of all things peaceful and tranquil.

Amian Bent

How to become a poet

When you wake up, look through every cotton strand that makes up your bed-sheet

with thorough circumspection to discover new spaces to stash your broken cries.

Gargle with a glass full of metaphors, similes, and hyperboles, but be prudent enough
to rinse out only the repetitive ones and allow the painful syllables to hole their way
into your stomach.

Eat a plateful of the heartbreak, depression, and battle wounds that dress your body
and hurl it all onto a piece of paper, for your grief is another person's art.

Take a walk every day, because you'll always be able to write about nature.

Don't ignore the scattered vowels on the sidewalk thrown away by somebody who
didn't know how to use them, pick them up to polish them into hymns that may even
worship the devil.

Don't be afraid to hand out those toffees filled with consonants, for there is nothing
better than being surrounded by more poets.

And if a friendly smile does come your way, stop writing and smile back, because they
might just open up another dimension for your art.

If you do manage to snag another human who's willing to be designated as your
significant other, make mental notes of everything they do.

Scribble down how each of their muscles moves when they're about to kiss you, and
how the two of you go on joyrides to chase the sunset.

And if they end up stabbing your heart, let yourself bleed every ounce of emotion that
you have ever felt into the palm of your hands and shove it between the lines. This way,
that ache will be visible to only those who have gone through it.

Never be afraid to catch the rainbow and put it in the glass bowl sitting on your stack of Bukowski's work. Never put your poetry on a leash from the fear of it consuming you, for the more restricted it gets, the smaller your head becomes.

Never hide your judgements in the margins because you think nobody can handle it.

Above all, never ever stop writing.

-Sampreeti Kale

<u>**THE ART OF WORDS**</u>

Most of my poems
smell of grief and
they have unlearnt
how to be hesitant
about it.

Usually, 'yesterday'
finds no meaning in them,
but 'tonight' throws
her turmoil over their head
like a soccer ball
dashing into the
opponent's goal.

my poems often
steal a tongue
from a lover's backyard
but refuses to mimic
his silence on heartbreaks.
The shrieks of the jet aircraft
captures their breath

for twice in a nanosecond
as if they're those fleeting birds
in search of a lost shelter,
so I thought of placing
my poems back in cages,
instead of capturing
someone else's freedom.
last summer, they chose
to camouflage on the
scruff of spring
like a broken vase
nourishing departures
almost back to life.
I think of some
old shredded memory,
they bring back nostalgia,
I think of perishing moments,
they bring back childhood,
I think of drenched love letters,
they bring back beloved's thirst,

my words, my thoughts

can never get enough

of illusive denials,

so most of my poems

have rusted in quest

of guarding warzones

where the flesh of

mustard fields

watched them

drink yellow blood,

where they bathed

in a stream of consciousness

that could merely interrupt

the poise of an earthed bride

learning to plant shrouds,

as she feels no one

comes back from the

pages of history

until recalled for once.

so they tried running away

and landed in a tunnel

their limbs went sick of separation

from a home they never knew,

although it was some redolence

dissolved in humanness

that could bind mortal love

in lifeless stars, often seen

pioneering an expanding yawn

of a fathomless cosmos,

where my poems unlearn

the language of Elysion and

lie on the deathbed of flowers

beheading fragrance while

floating over a sacrilegious brook.

- Mohua Chakraborty

About Poet/writer

An optimistic doer who sees the world with rose colored glasses and gets reflected in the introvertly reflecting spectra, who is fond of writing poems and instagram id goes as 'shayeri_i'

<u>**Memories**</u>

Some preserve their memories in a locker

like a treasure, and stare at them till their heart is full

while some carry a bundle of them on their shoulders

and never get tired and dull

some get used to it

while some makes remarkably stupid choices

and gets attached to it

It can make you smile, cry, bring tears of joy

and holds the ability, enough to make somebody coy

memories are infact like a jar of strawberry jam, the last

bite of your chocolate or may be a cup of cold coffee

once you get hold of it, its hard to let it go.

-Zaara Ali

<u>**The main character**</u>

From being the main character who is in a harmless love

who loves gazing out the window on a road trip.

Enjoying sad songs alone, and creating fake scenarios.

Who found love in a completely different person than them.

who would hang in to the hope of meeting them mid way

To being the main character, who has several crush online

But no one to share the warmth of their lovely sight who only can think about love,

and its a hypothetical situation for them

who is busy chasing their dreams, running around doing errands,

meeting friends, having work done, pampering themselves and mostly

LOVING THEMSELVES!!

-ZAARA ALI

<u>Summer love</u>

I read letters of my summer love,

"Immature madness" that's what he used to call!

"I wanna grow old with you,

and dance on streets in midnight,

I want to take you to a valley full of tulips,

to hum your favorite song, when the sun goes down.

You know what?

I will tell those silly flowers,

that I got one, prettier than all of you!

and you will smile, when I will hold your hand, tucking

your hair behind earlobe.

We'll lie down beneath the starry night, and I won't stop

adoring your cheeks,

I feel lucky to have you!

Someday, I will take you to a boat ride,

In a lake covered with maple leaves and swans,

and will recite to you then, the poem I wrote for you.

You will chuckle with tears.

Immature madness! Isn't it?

We'll build our home together, with bricks of love,

and then will adopt a dog.

I'll sit in the yard at evenings with you and will look into your eyes.

then you'll get to know, how much I love you.

I wanna grow old with you, and want to observe,

this immature madness, turning into love.

We will go for rides, and will dance on streets,

I will hold your hand in mine,

and seasons will change.

Your hair gonna turn grey, and my teeth will fall,

but we would be looking from the window,

how the sun goes down, in valley of tulips.

And me, reading the poem, I wrote for you!

Immature madness! Isn't it?

I read letters of my summer love,

and want you all to tell,

that I listen his poem twice a day.

And we have planted tulips in our garden.

My hair has turned grey, and his teeth have gone.

Sometimes when he moves to city,

I write him letters, and tell him that

this window feels incomplete without him.

I gaze at the sunset, and observe,

immature madness, turning into immense love.

With time as we grow older,

I wait for him, because he promises

To come back.

And he does.

I can identify his footsteps before he knocks the door,

he stands at the doorstep, and I scold him for being late,

then he moves his hand forward, and shows me,

the bouquet of tulips, he brought for me.

He further tucks my grey hair behind my earlobe,

looks in my eyes and says,

"Immature madness! Isn't it?"

And I smile, looking at him! ~

-Srishti

<u>**Stead**</u>

Life is meant to beckon you forward along the path

intended for you. Thoughts arise to show you something

about yourself and your life. It means something blissful

is waiting for you. You have lost sight of what you really

want. It's an opportunity to stimulate your curiosity.

It gives you a chance to connect with yourself.

Follow your heart and discover what matters most to you.

The harder we fight the way we are feeling, the harder it is to feel that way.

Accept what is, let go of what was and have hope in what will be.

Feeling lost isn't meant to stop you in your tracks.

Feeling uncertain and lost is part of your path.

See what those thoughts are showing you and embrace it.

Not until we are lost do we begin to understand ourselves.

If you don't like where you are, move.

Falling is what makes us grow, it makes us stronger and more resilient.

Thoughts can heal you.

Do not be afraid to lose yourself.

Think about what you want to do with your life.

Change happens in uncertainty.

It means shifting into something different and letting go some things.

When life isn't going your way, you have created the problem.

You are also the solution. You become what you think.

You will never be able to fix your life until you accept it is broken.

Find something you are great at and become perfect at it,

you will feel passionate about it.

When you know who you are, what you want, where you are going then nobody can stop you.

-Roopal Arora

Stoke

Life is meant to beckon you forward along the path intended for you. Thoughts arise to show you something about yourself and your life. It means something blissful is waiting for you. You have lost sight of what you really want. It's an opportunity to stimulate your curiosity. It gives you a chance to connect with yourself. Follow your heart and discover what matters most to you. The harder we fight the way we are feeling, the harder it is to feel that way. Accept what is, let go of what was and have hope in what will be. Feeling lost isn't meant to stop you in your tracks.

Feeling uncertain and lost is part of your path. See what those thoughts are showing you and embrace it. Not until we are lost do we begin to understand ourselves. If you don't like where you are, move. Falling is what makes us grow, it makes us stronger and more resilient. Thoughts can heal you.

Do not be afraid to lose yourself. Think about what you want to do with your life. Change happens in uncertainty. It means shifting into something different and letting go some things. When life isn't going your way, you have created the problem. You are also the solution. You become what you think. You will never be able to fix your life until you accept it is broken. Find something you are great at and become perfect at it, you will feel passionate about it. When you know who you are, what you want, where you are going then nobody can stop you.

-Roopal Arora

About Poet/writer

She is Roopal Arora. She has done engineering in Information Technology. She has done Masters in Business Administration in Information Technology. She is OCP and SAP professional. She has done two courses from British Council. She is Microsoft educator, buncee educator and wakelet educator. She is a brainmaths professional.She has 6 years experience in big IT firms like Wipro and CNEB network as IT professional. She is remotely working for Marucom private firm as Manager Technical.

Dandelions

Dandelions across the street

Kinda make me feel relieved

as the wind blows their petals

with a scent holding such beliefs

was i a fool to jump for one

Trying to keep hold of it

Cause i just cant take it

The bright colors shining at me

That made my days less of a pity

And less hard to breathe

To continue and be free

Like i always wanted to be as the yellow

sparks beneath my eyes

With a man made music in time

That gave me the comfort

I never had so if i get to pick a dandelion

I hope it won't be hard to pull

And easy to pick I hope i get to keep it

Until its petals begin to fall to keep

all its petals Until the day i get lost

So to my yellow dandelion

I hope i don't have to pick you out

And fly in my direction instead

For me to keep hold of you

And protect you like i never did.

-Dina Mohamed

<u>**The moon**</u>

I watched the moon

Let it ruin my mood

Cant stop thinking of you

When you were passing through

i looked and said

"Why did the moon had to ruin my mood?

When all i asked for was one afternoon?"

How can the moon turn

From the brightest ray above me

To the ray that burns me?

Every time i look at the moon

My eyes start to tear

My heart starts to ache

And i ask myself again

"How did the brightest moon become my darkest ray?"

I still think of the moon

Even if it's not there Cause once i looked at the moon

It seemed too close

Too close i have to let it go but the moon never leaves my mind

So i tell myself

"How can a moon cross ones mind like it was there every morning and noon?"

So if the moon sees this.

I hope i don't see you in my afternoons.

-Dina Mohamed

About Poet/writer

My name is dina im 16 years old im Egyptian and i recently got into poetry for the sake of writing feelings that cannot be described by others who are suffering from a mental illness or a dark time so maybe putting their feelings in words will help the world understand each other:)

<u>**An unfolded love**</u>

A page of beautiful distractions
pushing against my train of thoughts
like a cold morning
gently touching my soft wounds
How was your day?
Is your cat beside you right now?
Is she in your arms and clinging onto you?
Are you going through the mornings with a half-empty stomach?
Do you stay in bed and emptily stare at the ceiling?
Do you think of the past and the overwhelming future?
Do you think of the things that could and could not be?
I think I saw a stranger who looks like you today,
and it makes me think of you every second of the day.
And sometimes I wonder,
Do I ever cross your mind,
the way you cross mine?
Do you often dream about me,
the way I dream about you?
Do you often see me in the little things,
the way I see you in every creak against my wall?
What if I told you that the thought of your voice is keeping me up?
What if I told you that I've never held a hand like yours before?
That I've never met someone like you before?
What if I told you that your kiss still lingers on my lips?
that your honey-savored words echo in my head?
What if I told you that every part of you haunts me everyday?
That to love you is to destroy me?

Something about you keeps me hung up on you;
You're an album of memories that cost me my sanity-
We were an epitome of a bittersweet love;
we ran out of pages and froze in time,
but you were the stars in my sky and my home,
and I'll love you until the end of time.
And if my love for you was a question,
I'd spend the rest of my life answering every question.
-Sue Seth

<u>**I promised myself I'd never fall in love**</u>

I promised myself I would never fall in love,
and I'd grow weary every time
when I catch myself thinking of someone;
to have someone reside in my heart is my biggest fear,
and my deepest weaknesses.
But where is the lie?
I ended up sinking in love,
and now my heart is in my mouth,
and my stomach is tied in knots-
Where is the lie?
I saw a thousand galaxies in your eyes,
and I felt the galaxies collide
when your hands touched mine-
Where is the lie?
My tastebuds produce honey every time I say your name,
My eyes shine every time I spell your name,
and I dive in the universe like an astronaut
every time I see your eyes shine,
I dive in the deep sea every time I catch your scent.
Where is the lie?
I painted your name on my bones,
and you're the story that lingers in every line of my palm.
Where is the lie?
You're the room of art I'd visit every time,
you're the song I'd never grow tired of listening to,
you're the one whose eyes held mine,
you're the voice that comforts my heart,
the one who holds every part of me bare.
Where is the lie?
Every kiss of yours is a cursive line,
Every sound of yours is a different time-
And where is the lie?

I'd dance to the rhythm of your heart,
to the sound of your heartbeats,
and slowly I am withering in your love,
slowly I'm turning into just another translucent heart;
because my heart is a mess
and covered by bruises caused in the tears,
because I bleed in the nightfall,
and every touch of yours echoes through my mind.
And I promised myself I'd never fall in love,
and yet, I fell in love.
-Sue Seth

<u>June</u>
I'm homesick, yet I'm not sure what a home is-
June, do I call you my home?
Your name sounds like home; you feel like home.
I'd serenade your name endlessly
like a verse of a song tattooed all over my ribs,
like a verse of a poem stuck in my head.
We were an almost that almost happened
and in the end, I fell into pieces like a broken vase,
yet falling into pieces with you doesn't sound so bad;
to find the pieces of myself with you again.
This is the way it feels to me,
can you understand what I'm saying?
Does it feel this way to you?
Do you feel my heart on fire?
Was I broken for better?
You're a song that played with my heart strings;
like the sip of silence creaking in the middle of the night,
like the taste of my grief,
the color of my melancholy,
like the polaroids of the past etched into my heart,
like a stolen kiss I'd steal again-
Do you understand what I'm saying again?
So do I hold on or do I let go?
You left me on a burning ice,
and the embers of your touch are buried in my mind;
there's a chilling fire inside me
longing for this broken thread of hope
to become a once upon never,
to become a nothing and an everything,
to become an ocean of a happily never after.
-Sue Seth

<u>**Forbidden love**</u>
Is it a sin to write about her?
Is it a sin to write about the turns our fate took,
and the ache I feel at the thought of her?
Is it a sin to write about the way I forget the sky
when I see her smile?
About the way I see the universe in her eyes?
Is it a sin to write about the longing I feel,
and the warmth of her touch
that feels like a warm midnight spring?
Is it a sin to write about the things
that hold me back from facing her,
or looking through her eyes?
Is it a sin to write about the way
she gives me a warm fuzzy feeling in my chest
and makes me feel at home?
Or the way her voice comforts me
like a lullaby I'd endlessly listen to?
Or perhaps the way I'd serenade her name,
like a verse tattooed all over my ribs?
This month is full of metaphors,
and she's my biggest metaphor;
The stars whisper her name to me each night,
and she responds to me in my dreams,
and it goes through me
like a thread pierced by a needle;
and there's this formed hollowness in me
devouring me in silence,
until I'm left with nothing
but a few crumbled pieces of my heart
that long for nothing,
but the presence of her warmth.
-Sue Seth

About Poet/writer

Sue Seth, a 17-year-old poet and I've always wanted nothing more than having my poems published in a book. I've been writing for 5 years and the way poets see the world inspired me to write — I found writing as an outlet for my bottled emotions and unexpressed thoughts — and as time passed by I found more beauty in it, hence I decided to keep writing. And I hope, maybe in the soon future I'll get to publish my own books and have the world listen to my voice and unsaid words, and perhaps I'll get to publish poems together with my best friend, Dina too.

<u>**Mizzle**</u>

Often in the days of rain,
in my balcony;
I get lost in melancholy,
cherishing the moments with you.

The wind that passes by
has fragrance of your soul,
tiny drops falling
carries lost hopes.

Gazing at the sky
I close my eyes;
black clouds draping sun
holds parallel pain mine.

Array of light takes away
grief engraved deep inside heart;
tiny drops adhere sunlight,
bow averts from lamenting.

-Tanya Verma

Magic

They talked of

Those three magical words;

But perhaps,

Every word of yours was magical.

Believing magic to be just concealed in words,

I found it in every bit of yours;

Your love unfurling euphoria

That was something more magical.

Caring arms of yours

In which I could

Snuggle as a baby

Was magical.

And magical was the moment

When you decide to leave;

I perished

Everyday then!

- Tanya Verma

About Poet/writer

A teenager hailing from Gorakhpur. She's a bibliophile and creative writer. She has also co-authored anthologies and compiled them too.

Ad Astra

Broken teenagers, shattered dreams,

Counting to the farewell.

I hope you know, you had me at hello.

Bury our deepest despairs, save the tears, together.

Your hazel eyes are love reincarnated

I lose myself in its depths.

These screaming voices say,

I'm unworthy of your gaze.

Sculpting my fears so I can break them,

Your fingers drew constellations in the nape of my neck.

Made of glass, now with a purpose

Tell me how it feels to have a heartbeat.

Even if the end comes early,

Until the world falls away,

I carve this space for you out of myself.

Love me in lavender, so will I.

For the ocean has the moon,

And I have you.

-Nikitha Senny

<u>**Confessions**</u>

Dusty mirrors, blazing fires.

Burning lives and a clear looking glass,

Sparkly and shiny, now I see myself.

I have a confession to make you see.

The glass cracks, so does the image.

What do we see? The broken me. The real me.

Never wore a crown of sage leaves,

A coronet of ice it always was

Revelation after revelation,

The mirror now completely in pieces.

Illusions and lies broken apart,

Realities and lives embraced.

Determine your deepest desires,

The dancing shadows on the wall.

I walk away, god's favorite tragedy

Leaving behind that trapped infernal reflection.

-Nikitha Senny

About Poet/writer

Nikitha Senny is an 18-year-old aspiring writer and budding poet. Born and brought up in India, her academic interests lie in the field of Architecture and she is presently awaiting university acceptance.

Currently, she posts poems on her Instagram page @random_shades_of_pastel. She is grateful to have her poems as a medium of expression and also for the time spent creating them over the past 3 years. In her free time, she loves to journal, sketch and learn new things

Shah Jahan was a Birdcatcher

If love was a poem,

my mother says,

it would have no words.

because it is beyond the prettiest

of languages (ishq and ashq sound

so similar) and khusrau's riddles.

it would stabilize mir's mind

and burn ghalib's tongue.

you would carry it on your

shoulders without feeling

the weight of a feather.

love cannot be stored in a bell jar

or a grand architecture.

in love, you do not fall, you fly.

i believe that shah jahan

was a birdcatcher.

learning to hold a pencil

and a sword are two things.

the only similarity is both of them

are covered in blood.

the only difference is one of them

breathes blood in you,

the latter leads you to

the loss of it. if every artist has

to get his hands cut

for creating art,

the henna on mumtaz's palms

from the past

pities all the monuments

we will never open our eyes to.

i think taj is cursed

it sipped the blood of more than

twenty thousand people

yet came out colourless.

i shall smear my eyes in kohl

since so much light

pricks my eyeballs

and only darkness helps.

"i have hidden my thirst

from the vision of the sea,

wishing on the cloud that is

peeking through the gulmohar tree."

"pharaohs of our time

do not drown.

where did the people

who walked on water disappear?",

the flowers in the bagh whisper

to each other.

"then they told us

to breathe fondly,

but before that they

poisoned the air",

i hear the grave sing while

the quran verses stitched on

the marble walls echo through

intricate cupolas of the mahal

in throbbing silence.

taj mahal reminds me of

a birdcatcher poaching a starling,

instead of a dreamcatcher

hanging free.

it reminds me of grief

more than love.

raisins growing out of

fresh green grapes.

a giggling mouth trying to

swallow the lump in its throat.

why did mumtaz's death touch

shahjahan more than her

whole holy life could?

-Khatija Khan

Around the dear wish of thy heart,
Would entwine the cry of closure.
Lust, anger and sadness will sit verdantly still,
The fond charms of love will fade as they will.

As your bountiful eyes,
Blissed with joy that is unware of the truth that lies,
Loving is jeopardy in disguise.
Don't let them tell you otherwise,
On thy soul, its warm hands it lays,
The amorous bird of prey.

Love is a poem,
A poem of disobedience,
Where languish vows slowly clap power,
Where his eyes, his smile ensnare the obedience of the mind,
Where his words become the shadow of your truth behind.
In silent footsteps,
Betrayal creeps in.
And kills the love within.

Let thy cheeks be unprofaned by a tear,
And let your mind be void of any fears.
Yet by heaven, I think your love is rare,
Don't be belied by false compare.

Thaw your heart while the eternal wind sings,

Thou shall see very soon the sky of spring.

Where the warmth of the sun kisses you with serenity,

And you taste the love of eternity

- Hridya sharma

About Poet/Writer

Belief is the elixir of dreams, is it not? Dreams define the very existence of a man's being. I am Hridya Sharma, in three simple words, I would like to describe myself as a dreamer, achiever, and believer. I believe in the power to achieve your aims lies within you. Experience – Writing has always been my passion. In my 1.5 years of content writing, I have written blogs, articles, stories, poems, social media captions, pr messages, and emailers. The search for creative endeavors has never stopped and it has only made me realize that in the game of writing, no matter how many milestones you achieve or stories you write, it gives the feeling of writing as much as you can. Honestly being an author, storyteller and public speaking enthusiast, all the pieces of content I create are the stories that I want to tell, the lessons I want people to learn, and tales that I want people to get inspired by.

Dear fluffy, my confidante and dearest friend for life,

People think I'm insane for mourning your loss after 8 years

and still being as aggrieved as I was.

I remember the day you left me, June 11th, I've never forgotten the day or the time.

When I returned home and locked myself in my room,

Buried my head in the comfort of my bed's plush Cushions and thick sheets.

Snuggled under the blanket and felt half-alive, numb and paralysed.

The sunlight streaming in through the window, but unable to dispel

the melancholy greyness that surrounded me.

Maybe I shouldn't remember those moments.

Aside from the sense of your presence and the false nostalgia,

That leads me to believe differently.

Your embrace would resurrect the dead soul inside me.

Your gentle meows would kindle a small fire beneath my tortured soul.

And tell me that maybe I'm not useless, that maybe I have a purpose,

That I can make a difference in someone's life.

The clinking of the small cookies being poured into your metal dish,

While you sat attentively, gaze concentrated on the treat, head lowered,

Your hairy paws brushing the chilly container's edge,

Observing you satiate your hunger and then crawl next me,

Purring softly with your eyes partially closed,

Occasionally sticking out your cherry red tongue to

Scratch your white as snow body,

While I frowned at your blind faith in me,

How did you find it so simple?

I used to converse with you for hours and find refuge

And comfort in your gentle acknowledgement.

As if you understood my words and felt exactly what I felt,

Or perhaps that's what I convinced myself of over time,

I would rant to you and release the volcano of my rage,

Exposing everyone who harmed me, exploited me and let it all out.

Remember when i told you about her bitter attitude?

I'm sure you despised her as well.

You and I were inseparable on the days when i fell sick,

As if to reassure me that everything will be fine,

And when i recovered, you were overjoyed,

We raced and played and danced yelled as we wandered around the park.

Everything seemed so lovely that day, except for the time that flew by so quickly.

I wish things had turned out the same when you became sick,

I still feel your tickle now and then, and my tears well up a bit

When i think of your innocent face,

Sparkling blue eyes and blush pink nose.

People make fun of me, but how can I tell them?

I lost a bit of me, a memory that I will treasure forever.

An extract from my past, a personification of my darkest moments,

A reflection of my greatest difficulties,

A piece of myself and who I am.

-Sani zehra

About Poet/writer

Hi, I am Sani Zehra (Saa-ni). Writing poems has been my hobby since childhood, and I throughly enjoy expressing my emotions and manifesting my thoughts using poetry as a medium. It allows me to be creative and gives me a free hand to knit and intertwine my thoughts and words into something personal and close. This poem is about the loss of a pet— man's greatest companion, in my opinion. It reflects loss, and the many ways in which the absence and presence of a pet can affect your life that I'm sure most owners can relate to, including myself, which is what makes it so special.

<h1 style="text-align:center"><u>The new normal</u></h1>

 I wake up to the sound of buzzing horns and the pitter patter of raindrops on my window.

Today's a Sunday.

I tuck myself under the sheets and try to get myself back to sleep..go back to the dream that i was having.

The dream where maa braids my hair while reciting stories

She used to hear from grandma in her long lost childhood,

the dream where my father kisses me on the forehead

and tries to get me out of the bed on early mornings,

the dream where my siblings used to come finish the savory glass of milk maa had just served for me to have and how i used to chase them for all their mischiefs.

that was MY normal. but it's not the same now,is it?..

 "what i have now is my new normal."

I finally get up from my bed half heartedly and take a glance around me.

It's been almost a year since I've shifted to the city for my higher studies.

Maa said it will be worth it, but somehow i always find myself longing to go back,always find myself at a loss when it comes to adjusting myself with this new normal.

oh how desperately i wish i could go back to what i had earlier, run along the rice fields in our village, lie down at the shade of the banyan tree on summer afternoons and feel the cool breeze on my face.

Everything is so different here.
The skies don't look the same anymore,
The sunsets in our village used to be tinted with pretty crimson red and orange hues,
while all i get here is pale, dull sunsets.
Back in our village, the moon and i used to have conversations every night,
while here all i do is stare across my window pane at the citylights.

The past year has not at all been all sweet and savory for me.
Uncountable memories I have left behind, indescribable moments of love and
happiness i wish i could feel again, adjusting to a new environment was never a piece
of cake for me but then adjusting to the new normal is all that life really is isn't it?

I lazily open my laptop as i take a bite of the sandwich leftover from yesterday..
another thing to remind me of how pampered i was at home, how maa never let me
go outside the house without having a proper breakfast.
Cut to the present, ironically I'm living off of stale and leftover food for almost a year
now..just because no matter whatever expensive food I order it never tastes like how
maa's food does..

I surf the net for a few hours but my mind just can't get focused so i decide to just give
up and lay down on my bed as I patiently wait for brighter rainbows and warmer
skies to adorn my days,
I reminisce all the prettiest moments I've left behind at my home that I'd die to live
again,
All the silliest fights I'd love to fight again and all the hopeless crushes i had when i
was young, that I'd love to fall for again..

I can slowly sense myself drift away to sleep as these words that maa and paa uttered
to keep ringing in my ears -
"live for what tomorrow can bring, not what yesterday has taken away"

-P.R augustina Mahanta

<u>**"My sunshine in human form"**</u>

Pink cherry blossoms adorn the beautiful sight before you as you softly lay down with your beloved on the subtly wet grass, fingers intertwined; you take a smooth quick glance of your love as the sunrays kiss their coffee coloured cheeks and deep brown eyes, what have i done to deserve an angel like you love?

Calm waves slightly kiss your feet as you tiptoe around while dancing on the beach with your beloved; a slight breeze ruffles and plays with your hair as all you can hear are the adorable giggles you both utter as you run along the shore ~

-P.R augustina Mahanta

About Poet/writer

Hey everyone ! Augustina this side! I am a 20 year old student currently pursuing my Bachelor's degree in Science Stream. I am currently a resident of Assam and the two things my heart broods over always are writing and singing. Writing and music in any form are what makes me feel alive and joyful in my monotonous life. I hope to bring comfort to people through my writing and my voice when i sing.

I long to walk a hundred million steps,

Till I get surrounded by an Oak grove,

Till i hear the wheeze of conch played by a gentle

Zephyr above an icy sea,

Till i come across an abandoned

Hut with wooden furniture

Sprinkled with glimmering dust,

Till I find the three witches upon heath and dormouse

At a mad tea party,

And after this, I long to walk a hundred million steps.

-Sarab bawa

This universe and us

1) This universe is a spherical ball where we are faces made in round circles. I have been told the timezones are different; every country has a time like how we have different accents. Names sit on the tip of my tongue and they stay there till I learn how to pronounce one. I will eventually learn how to live too.

2) My universe is a box, in four quarters and I come back to it again and again to make a memory because it takes 15 seconds to make one. It took 4.5 billion years to form an earth and our brain just takes 15 seconds to make a memory.
How many it made and how many it broke; looking at my fingers that writes a poem, this looks like another promise of mine.
3) The washing machine looks like the revolving earth where different people are holding onto each other, your shirt hugging the corner of my uniform, my hello owning a part in your goodbyes.
Us is a shorter version of calling each other universe.

3) Our throat speaks languages in different mother tongues but stays in only one place because we belong to one. This universe is a big throat with a voice that sounds like a hiccup.
Hiccup that's heard even after someone leaves, a hiccup
that you can store even after it stopped because this universe does the same too.

4) Universe is a person, maybe we never know it resembles.
This is us, we never know we are an universe that never resides in one place.

-Sharli

Guilt

Guilt is an ache in your throat, it fears coming out so chooses to stay,

Like a red banana in the plate of yellow bananas, guilt carries along with it a difference always,

For me, guilt is a room where I moved along

And didn't step out because there were too many in the room; trying to escape the same.

Guilt is a person who shares the same name but doesn't want to have an identity, so they form a part in life.

Until we die, guilt lives.

Maybe, grief chooses to be in a person instead of being a person.

-Sharli

<u>**The world of Hicks and Slobs**</u>

An ordinary mind; an ordinary day.

Of how the eyes shy away

Amid a whirlpool of said things.

They claim to be clear

Blame for being unfair

Cat call the cat.

Nothing new; nothing much.

Of tired hands in dawn of spring.

They call for hues; so queer

Green of summers

Fading winter trees

Seasons are unfolding.

Last words; lost wills.

Of lovers who seldom meet.

They promise land

Aim for the skies

Hand in hand

Full of lies.

A heart speaks.

-Kajal

Are you dreaming to be a published author? Kick start your writing carrier by publishing your own book. Don't spend hefty amount on publishing your book. We have excellent offers for you.

If you want to edit, design or publish your own book email us
pentupthoughts4@gmail.com

Our publishing package starts from Rs. 499 Kindle Ebook

Rs. 1499(without book cover) and Rs.1999(with book cover) Paperback only

Rs.2999 paperback with book cover+ Ebook(promotion on pentupthoghts)

www.ingramcontent.com/pod-product-compliance
Lightning Source LLC
Chambersburg PA
CBHW031634170726
47990CB00017B/1013